Random Kindness & Senseless Acts of Beauty

Written by Anne Herbert & Margaret Paloma Pavel

Illustrated by Mayumi Oda

Foreword by Desmond Tutu

New Village Press, New York

Published by
New Village Press
New York, NY 10025
www.newvillagepress.org

New Village Press is a nonprofit, public-benefit publisher.
Our books are distributed by New York University Press.

Printed in China

This is the 30th Anniversary Edition.
Publication Date: April 2024

Cataloguing is available through the Library of Congress.

ISBN 9781613322284

Foreword

We are living in an historic moment. We are each called to take part in a great transformation. Our survival as a species is threatened by global warming, economic meltdown, and an ever-increasing gap between rich and poor. Yet these threats offer an opportunity to awaken as an interconnected and beloved community.

Here in South Africa, interconnectedness is described by the concept *ubuntu*. Ubuntu is the philosophy and belief that our humanity is inextricably bound up in one another, and any tear in the fabric of connection must be repaired for us all to be made whole. This interconnectedness is the very root of who we are. Thus, compassion and service to others enhances the humanity of all, including oneself. As South Africa overcame the trauma of Apartheid, we discovered that ubuntu builds extraordinary resilience, enabling our people to survive and emerge still human despite all efforts to dehumanize our community.

Ubuntu tells us that we can create a more peaceful world by striving for goodness in each moment, wherever we are. Thus we are invited to become life artists, those who create lives of wholeness and beauty at every instant. Out of the cacophony of random suffering and chaos that can mark human life, the life artist sees or creates a symphony of meaning and order. A life of wholeness does not depend on what we experience, but on how we experience our lives.

My conviction that this is true is borne out not only by my experiences in South Africa, where we miraculously averted a bloodbath by cultivating forgiveness over cycles of retribution and violence, but also by many visits to other countries suffering oppression and conflict. We can indeed transform the world, and we are each called to take part in this sacred work.

Random Kindness and Senseless Acts of Beauty offers this simple and powerful message of wisdom and hope. Wherever we are, we can create beauty. Moment by moment, we can create joy. Instant by instant, we can offer kindness.

—Desmond Mpilo Tutu, Soweto, 2014

Random Kindness & Senseless Acts of Beauty

Our leaders got confused.

So . . .

we're all leaders now.

They told us there
was nothing we
could do.

They were wrong.

When we
tell ourselves
there is
nothing we
can do,

We are wrong.

We never know how much,
and we never know how far it goes,

But always
we have power.

We have power

We're all making the soup
we're all eating.

We're all weaving the cloth
we're all wearing.

What we do can't go away.

We are all in the circle together.

Anything we do randomly
and frequently

Starts to make
its own sense

And changes the world
into itself.

Senseless violence makes

more and more sense,

when vengeance and fear

*Take us
closer and
closer to a world
where everyone
is dead
for no reason.*

But violence isn't the only thing
that is senseless

until it makes its own sense.

Anything you want there to be more of,

Do it randomly.

Don't wait for reasons.

It will make itself
be more
senselessly.

Scrawl it on the wall—

Random Kindness and Senseless Acts of Beauty!

*We are right on the edge
of discovering
millions of new ways
of being together,*

*Millions of
new dances*

*we can
do together
minute by minute.*

And we're right on the edge of destroying ourselves out of life,

Because we are too scared to have that much delight.

We're right on the edge.

The steps we take now
make new earth grow
beneath our feet.

The steps
we take now
decide
what kind
of earth that
will be.

*In every moment
we live
we have the choice*

to find the fight
or make
delight.

We have Power.

It's a circle.

Start the dance.

The first edition of this book was published to break the spell of war, random violence, and senseless acts of cruelty. Now, our commonwealth of earth, air, and water are seriously threatened, and the call to link arms and lay down armaments is more urgent than ever. Together we can make a new earth grow.

I am grateful Anne Herbert's phrase from 1982—Practice random kindness and senseless acts of beauty—has proliferated worldwide. It is a testament to her poetic wisdom. May you take to heart the message that every action makes a difference in an inextricably connected world.

—*M. Paloma Pavel, Oakland, California*

When Anne Herbert and Margaret Paloma Pavel approached me to illustrate this beautiful story, I had been working as an antinuclear activist in Japan and the United States. I felt strongly drawn to this message and poured my emotions onto the images, creating a pictorial complement that drew from my experiences with our world and my work as an activist. I based my design on the 12th Century Japanese scroll—*Birds and Animals Frolicking*.

My original art for the book was painted in black and red. In early 2011, I felt compelled to turn my illustrations into color, breathing new life into the story. I was deeply immersed in this venture when the tragic earthquake and tsunami struck on March 11, 2011. I was in Nara, Japan, at that time working with traditional scroll-maker Mr. Shosaku Yoshimura. It was there I knew this timely story had to be told, once again, to the new generations that will care for this planet.

I dedicate this scroll to every child of the Earth.

—*Mayumi Oda, Kealakekua, Hawaii*

This Thirtieth Anniversary Edition of *Random Kindness* is dedicated to peace and recovery in the face of world unrest and climate crises.

Anne Herbert was an American writer and assistant editor of *CoEvolution Quarterly*. She is known for authoring the expression, "Practice random kindness and senseless acts of beauty."

Margaret Paloma Pavel is an educator, psychologist, and international advocate of healthy, just, and resilient urban communities. She is founder and president of Earth House Center in Oakland, California, and editor of *Breakthrough Communities: Sustainability and Justice in the Next American Metropolis.*

Mayumi Oda is a global activist and revered artist known as the "Matisse of Japan." She has illustrated the books of the esteemed Buddhist monk Thich Nhat Hanh and exhibited over fifty one-woman shows throughout the world. She is the author of seven books, including *I Opened the Gate, Laughing.*

Desmond Mpilo Tutu was Archbishop Emeritus of Cape Town South Africa and a world renowned social rights activist. He was recipient of the Nobel Peace Prize, the Albert Schweitzer Prize for Humanitarianism, the Pacem in Terris Award, the Sydney Peace Prize, and the Gandhi Peace Prize.